The Performers

By Julia Nasser
Illlustrated by Erin Eitter Kono

"There is nothing to do," whined Maria for the thirteenth time that morning.

Her twin sister Carmen ignored her. Maria's whining was endless.

"I am so bored. This is the dullest place on Earth!"

Carmen had heard Maria say this many times. Now Carmen closed her book and looked at her restless sister.

"What would you like to do?" Maria asked. "We could go outside. Or maybe grandma would help us bake cookies?"

Maria was never silent. She never sat still. She squirmed wildly on the sofa.

"Maria," Carmen said, "I have a great idea."

"What?" Maria asked in a hopeless tone.

"Let's put on skits. We can write the lines. We can get costumes and props from the attic. We can organize and direct skits. Then we can perform them."

"That is a silly idea," grumped Maria.

"Is it any sillier than sitting on the couch and whining? We can ask our friends to help," Carmen said.

Carmen asked her friend Bill to help her. She thought he was funnier than most comics on TV.

Maria asked her friend John to be her partner. He was a skillful artist. He was sure to have good ideas.

The attic was crammed with junk. It was a
great place to explore. Wonderful things lurked in
the darkness.

The children pulled out worn shirts, purses,
and scarves for costumes. They dragged out old
pots and dishes for props.

Then they sat down to write the lines for
their skits.

Carmen and Bill used the story of *Little Red Riding Hood* for their skit. An old purse was the picnic basket. A blanket was Red Riding Hood's cape.

Bill was the Wolf. He was very funny. Bill was a great sneaky wolf. Carmen moved gracefully on the stage. Her long cape swirled around her.

Maria and John based their skit on *King Arthur and His Knights.* Their set was a king's throne.

Maria was a knight. John was King Arthur. John made a coat of armor out of cardboard for Maria. Their skit had lots of running, jumping, and yelling. They were excited about their skit.

After dinner the children performed the skits for their families. When they finished, everyone clapped loudly. It was a very successful event.

Later that night, Carmen and Maria were in their beds tired from their busy day.

"That was a lot of fun!" Maria said. "So, what are we going to do tomorrow?"